Build Your Own
Secret
Bookcase Door

By Daniel Berg

Copyright © 2010
ISBN: 1453760814
EAN-13: 9781453760819

The Complete Guide with detailed plans for building your own Secret Bookcase Door.

Secret Bookcase Door

www.homesafetytoday.net

Digital images courtesy Aaron Hirsh

Every family can use a safe room. A place in the home to retreat to in an emergency. Wouldn't it be great if the kids had a secret place to hid during a home invasion or burglary. Now you can utilize these attractive built in designed book cases to act as a hidden door into any area. These doors are available from a variety of custom manufacturers or can be built by anyone with basic handy man skills. We have worked out all of the tricks that allow the bookcase to swing open yet still look like a custom built in cabinet when closed.

We were in the middle of a kitchen and dinning room remodel when we decided to close off the kitchen hall entrance. This decision resulted in a long hallway to nowhere. I wanted to use the space for storage but my wife refused have a closet door in her dinning room. After a google search and some time online we found the perfect solution a secret hidden bookcase door. This way the unit would look like a built in cabinet from the Dinning Room and would still allow access to the storage space behind. The only problem was price. Basic starting price for a Bookcase door is over $2500.00 and that does not include over $400 in P&H or instillation. To make a long story short I called a friend who worked as a cabinet maker and together we designed this simple to construct yet professional looking swing in painted Bookcase Door that can be built by anyone with minimal woodworking skills and a few basic tools. Best of all my Bookcase Door ended up costing less than $300 including all wood, screws, primer, paint and brushes. The bookcase displayed in these plans was designed to fit the rough opening in my wall. Height and width dimensions can be changed to meet your own requirements but remember that you may have to adjust spacing to allow the door to swing properly. Basically, if you build the bookcase door as designed it will swing open properly but if you change any dimensions (especially depth) it is recommended to do the math to assure the box will still swing open. Unlike other Bookcase Door designs which require expensive pivot hinges and elaborate tools our design incorporates standard door hinges and is designed for the average homeowner to build.

The Complete Guide with detailed plans for building your own Secret Bookcase Door.

Secret Bookcase Door

www.homesafetytoday.net

This Bookcase door is designed to swing in. The simple solution that allows this design to work is using a standard 2x4 wall construction on the swinging side while using a 2 x 8 support on the hinge side. With the hinge mounted on the back side this design allows the bookcases forward edge to clear the frame when opening. Sounds complicated but its really a simple alternative to other complicated designs and also eliminates the need for expensive speciality hinges. All you have to do is make sure spacing listed below is duplicated.

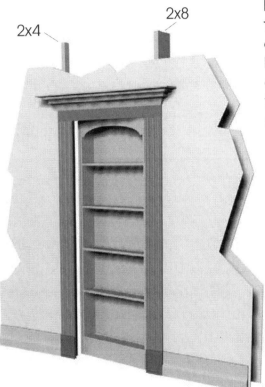

2x4   2x8

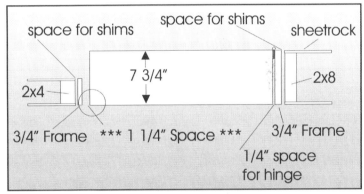

space for shims   space for shims   sheetrock

7 3/4"

2x4

2x8

3/4" Frame   *** 1 1/4" Space ***   3/4" Frame

1/4" space for hinge

Top View Door Closed View shows spacing required to allow box to swing open.

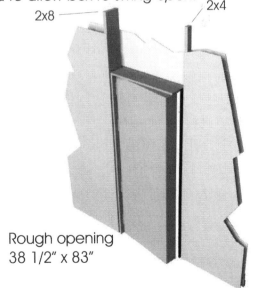

2x8   2x4

Rough opening 38 1/2" x 83"

Top View Door Open. Shows min clearance at back edge of 2x4

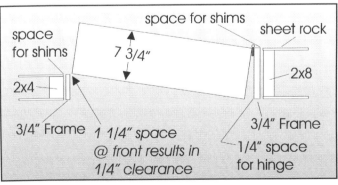

space for shims   sheet rock

space for shims

7 3/4"

2x4

2x8

3/4" Frame   1 1/4" space @ front results in 1/4" clearance   3/4" Frame

1/4" space for hinge

Secret Bookcase Door
www.homesafetytoday.net

Please note that the cabinet for this project is designed to display a variety of photo frames, statues and other ornate objects. If you plan to stock the shelves with heavy books the hinges and construction may have to be reinforced.

Image #2 Right: Bookcase door in closed position with molding in place hiding seams and creating the effect of a built in cabinet.

Image #2

Image #3

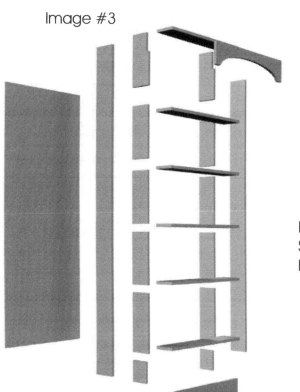

Image #3 Left:
Shows a breakdown of components for the bookcase portion of this project.

The Complete Guide with detailed plans for building your own Secret Bookcase Door.

Secret Bookcase Door

www.homesafetytoday.net

The Bookcase Door is constructed from 3/4 inch furniture grade finished both side Birch plywood. I had two 4 x 8 sheets striped to 7 3/4". In addition 1/4 Finished both side plywood is used for the back and a variety of molding can be used to make the unit look like its built into the wall.

Tools Required:

Chop saw or circular saw
Table saw
Jig saw
Screw Gun
Hammer
Level
Wood Glue
Wood file
Razor knife
Iron
1 1/4 screws
2" screws
3" screws
finishing nails
Wood putty
Putty knife
Sand paper
White Primer
Paint

Bookcase Construction:

Unless you have a quality table saw I would highly recommend going to the local lumber yard and having two 4' x 8'x 3/4 furniture grade plywood ripped into 7 3/4" x 8' strips. You can also have a 4' x 8' x 1/4 sheet ripped down to finished size for the back. This simple step will save a lot of time plus it assures that all of the 7 3/4' pcs are perfect matches. All you have to do now is cut each to length, cut a couple notches and begin construction.

The Complete Guide with detailed plans for building your own Secret Bookcase Door.

Secret Bookcase Door
www.homesafetytoday.net

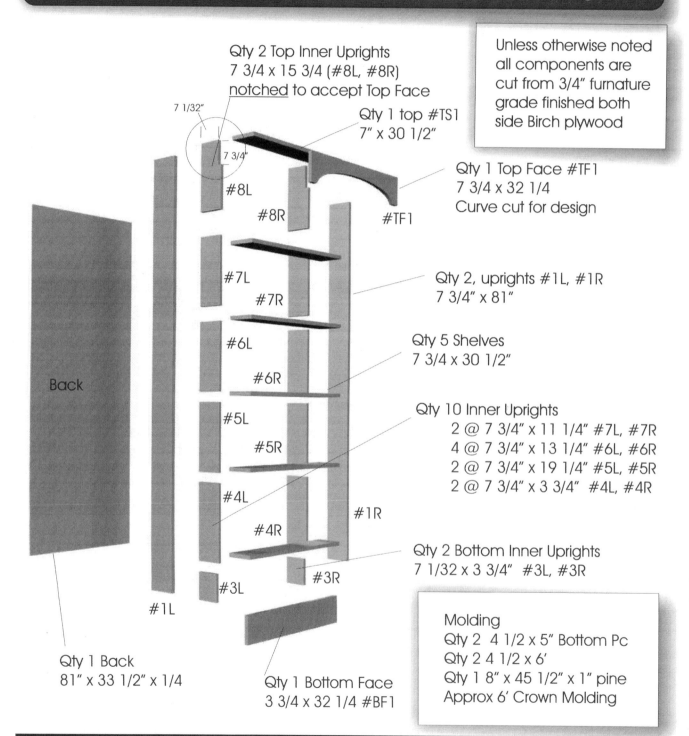

Qty 2 Top Inner Uprights
7 3/4 x 15 3/4 (#8L, #8R)
<u>notched</u> to accept Top Face

7 1/32"

7 3/4"

#8L

#8R

Qty 1 top #TS1
7" x 30 1/2"

Unless otherwise noted
all components are
cut from 3/4" furnature
grade finished both
side Birch plywood

Qty 1 Top Face #TF1
7 3/4 x 32 1/4
Curve cut for design

#TF1

#7L

#7R

Qty 2, uprights #1L, #1R
7 3/4" x 81"

#6L

#6R

Qty 5 Shelves
7 3/4 x 30 1/2"

Back

#5L

#5R

Qty 10 Inner Uprights
2 @ 7 3/4" x 11 1/4" #7L, #7R
4 @ 7 3/4" x 13 1/4" #6L, #6R
2 @ 7 3/4" x 19 1/4" #5L, #5R
2 @ 7 3/4" x 3 3/4" #4L, #4R

#4L

#4R

#1R

Qty 2 Bottom Inner Uprights
7 1/32 x 3 3/4" #3L, #3R

#3L

#3R

#1L

Qty 1 Back
81" x 33 1/2" x 1/4

Qty 1 Bottom Face
3 3/4 x 32 1/4 #BF1

Molding
Qty 2 4 1/2 x 5" Bottom Pc
Qty 2 4 1/2 x 6'
Qty 1 8" x 45 1/2" x 1" pine
Approx 6' Crown Molding

Step #1
Cut all wood for bookcase to length.

Step #2
Attach Inner Uprights #3L through #8L to Upright #1L leaving a 3/4" space between each. Note that Inner Upright length can be changed to create different shelf heights. Measurements provided are sizes we used on our project. Place #1L on flat surface. Working from bottom to top, glue and use two 1 1/4 finishing nails to secure each Inner Upright in place. **Use a scrap of 3/4 plywood between each Inner Upright so that you end up with the required 3/4" space that will support each shelf. Inner Upright #3L will have to be flush with back edge of Upright #1L. All others will mount flush with the front edge. Once all uprights are in place, pre-drill holes for two screws in each slot. Next turn over #1L and use 1 1/4" screws to secure each inner upright permanently. Inner upright #8L must be notched to accept Top Face . The best way to do this is to hold Top Face into place then and mark notch. All edges of plywood will be finished with edging. This means that the Top Face board should mount slightly higher (approx 1/32") than front edge of #8L. I cut a small pc of edging and held it into position before marking #8L for notch. Cut the same notch for #8R

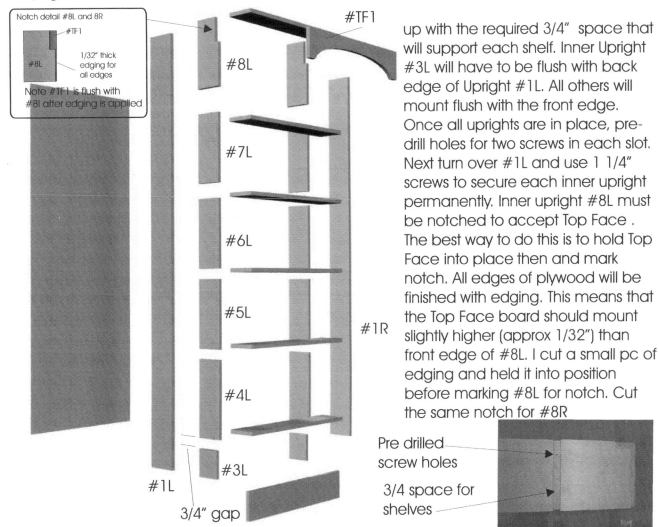

Notch detail #8L and 8R

#TF1

#8L

1/32" thick edging for all edges

Note #TF1 is flush with #8l after edging is applied

#TF1

#8L

#7L

#6L

#5L

#4L

#3L

#1L

#1R

3/4" gap

Pre drilled screw holes

3/4 space for shelves

The Complete Guide with detailed plans for building your own Secret Bookcase Door.

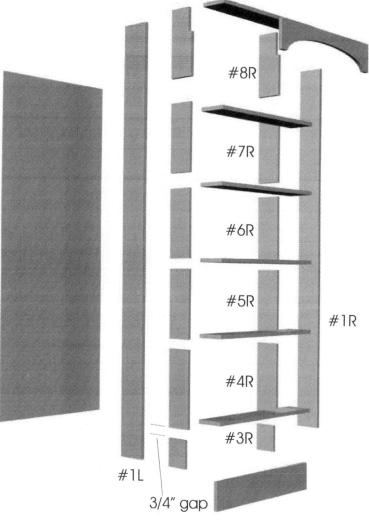

Step #3 (repeat for R side)
Attach Inner Uprights #3R through #8R to Upright #1R leaving a 3/4" space between each. Place #1L on flat surface. Working from bottom to top glue and use two 1 1/4 finishing nails to temporarily secure each Inner Upright in place. **Use a scrap of 3/4 plywood between each Inner Upright so that you end up with the required 3/4" space that will accept shelf. Once all uprights are in place turn over #1R and use 1 1/4" screws to secure each inner upright to #1R.

Step #4

With both uprights now assembled its time to mount shelves into place. On a flat surface place each shelf into 3/4 slots of Upright #1L. Two 2" screws and a little wood glue can be used to secure each. Make sure front edge of each shelf is flush with front edge of Upright #1L

Secret Bookcase Door

www.homesafetytoday.net

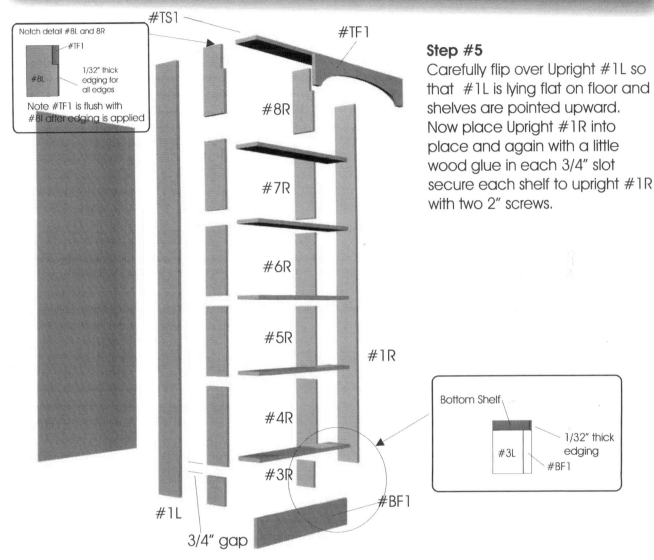

Notch detail #8L and 8R

#TF1

#8L

1/32" thick edging for all edges

Note #TF1 is flush with #8l after edging is applied

#TS1

#TF1

#8R

#7R

#6R

#5R

#1R

#4R

#3R

#BF1

#1L

3/4" gap

Bottom Shelf

1/32" thick edging

#3L

#BF1

Step #5

Carefully flip over Upright #1L so that #1L is lying flat on floor and shelves are pointed upward. Now place Upright #1R into place and again with a little wood glue in each 3/4" slot secure each shelf to upright #1R with two 2" screws.

Step #6

Use wood glue and finishing nails secure Bottom Face # BF1 to #3L, #3R and bottom shelf. Make sure that front edge of bottom shelf is flush with Bottom Face #BF1 (see image above). I used the same small pc of edging and held it in place before securing #BF1 in place. #BF1 should then be secured to #1L and #1R with 2" screws.

Step #7

Use wood glue and finishing nails secure Top Face # TF1 to #8L, #8R and top shelf #TS1. Make sure that front edge of #TF1 is approx 1/32"higher than front edge of #8L and 8R. This will allow all surfaces to be flush once edging is added to exposed plywood edges. I used the same small pc of edging and held it in place before securing #BF1 in place.

The Complete Guide with detailed plans for building your own Secret Bookcase Door.

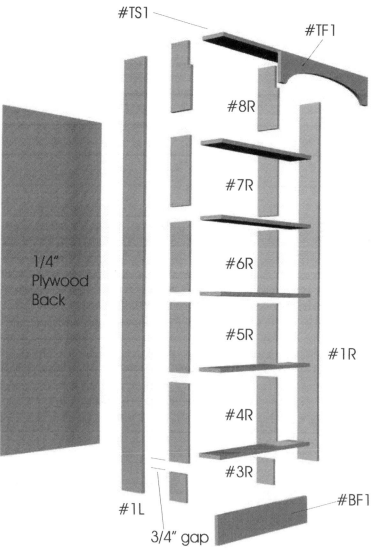

#TS1

#TF1

#8R

1/4"
Plywood
Back

#7R

#6R

#5R

#1R

#4R

#3R

#1L

#BF1

3/4" gap

Step #8

secure 1/4" plywood back to bookcase with wood glue and finishing nails. Measure from top R corner to Bottom L corner and confirm box is square before securing back in place. You should get the same measurement as from top L to Bottom R. If box is out of square it can still be tilted. Once secured the 1/4" back will hold book case square.

Secret Bookcase Door
www.homesafetytoday.net

Step #9

Wood Edging can be added to all unfinished edges. First sand all edges with a block. Edging is applied with a standard home iron. Edging length can be cut with a razor knife. After cooling, edging width is then striped with a corse file and downward motion. After the edging is applied you will have to lightly sand then fill any gaps in edging with wood putty. This is a good time to putty all screw and nails holes. Once the putty is dry the bookcase will need sanding and possibly another application of putty before its ready to be primed and painted.

Note: Bookcase Box can now be places in rough opening of wall. Use shims to level box. If floor is not level bottom of Box can be scribed and cut to make a perfect fit. Just use a pc of 1/4" wood held flat on the floor and scribe a line across front face. Box was designed with a raised bottom shelf to allow for trim.

Image shows sample of wood edging. Edging is approx 1/32 thick and is applied to all exposed plywood edges with a standard home iron.

Bottom edge can be scribed and cut if floor is uneven.

The Complete Guide with detailed plans for building your own Secret Bookcase Door.

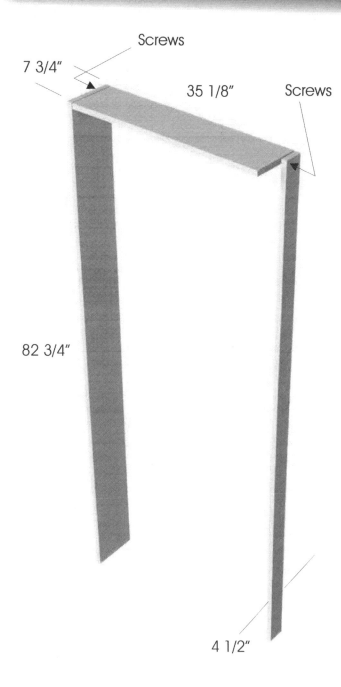

Screws

7 3/4"

35 1/8"

Screws

82 3/4"

4 1/2"

Step #10

Once the Bookcase is finished its time to create a simple frame for the door. This frame will be mounted to back edge of bookcase with hinges then mounted into rough opening in wall with shims and wood screws. Side and top can be cut from the same 7 3/4 x 3/4 plywood strips used to build bookcase box. The third side (side mounted to 2x4) will have to be striped to size with a table saw.
Once all pcs are cut secure each with wood glue and 2" screws as shown.

Note: Only 3 pcs. Do not make bottom.

Attach hinge to door with 1 1/4 screws

Step #11
Hinges can be attached to back edge of Bookcase box as shown. Two hinges should be mounted toward top of box for extra strength. If you plan on using the bookcase for heavy books rather than decorative items it may require additional hinges.

Step #12
Attach hinges to back side of 7 3/4 with sill. Bottom edge of frame should be 1/4 " lower than bottom edge of Bookcase. (this space prevents bookcase from rubbing on floor.
It is very important that front edge of frame is even with front edge of bookcase.

Note: It is easier to use temporary 1" screws to secure hinges to frame. Once the frame and door combination are mounted into rough opening of wall, these short screws should be replaced with 3" screws.

Secret Bookcase Door

www.homesafetytoday.net

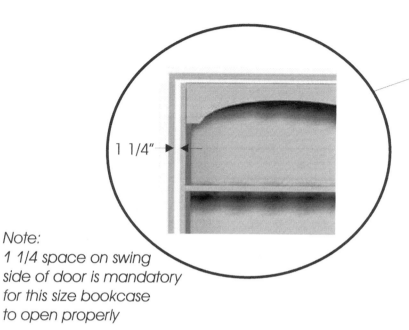

1 1/4"

Note:
*1 1/4 space on swing
side of door is mandatory
for this size bookcase
to open properly*

Step #13

With bookcase box attached to frame its
time to insert entire pc into rough opening
of wall. Frame side with hinges should be
shimmed and mounted first. Make sure
front edge is flush with front edge of wall.
Entire frame can then be shimmed and
mounted flush to wall.

Now is the time to test if bookcase door
swings freely.

Secret Bookcase Door

www.homesafetytoday.net

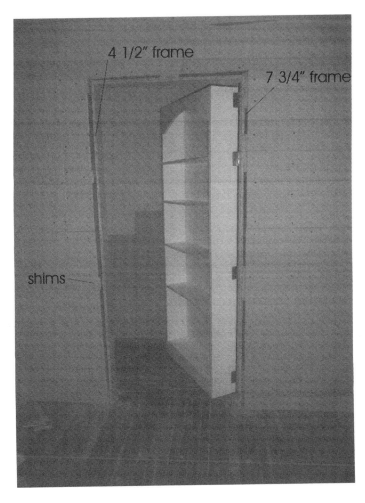

4 1/2" frame

7 3/4" frame

shims

Bookcase door mounted to frame and seured in place. Molding will be added to creat the illusion of a built in cabinet

Note placement of hinges at back of bookcase box. Hinges are attached to bookcase with 1 1/4 screws and to the wall with 3" screws.

Note hinges are mounted to back edge of Bookcase door and Back of
7 3/4" plywood frame.

The Complete Guide with detailed plans for building your own Secret Bookcase Door.

Secret Bookcase Door

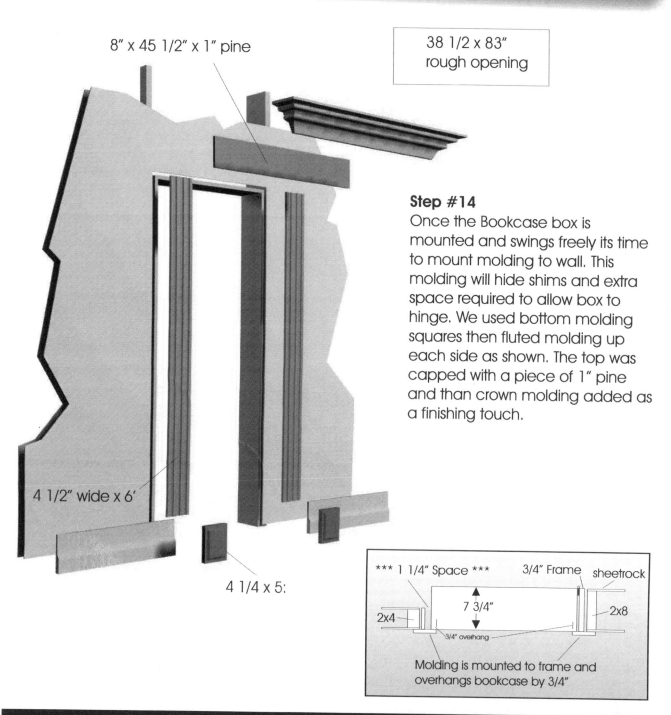

8" x 45 1/2" x 1" pine

38 1/2 x 83"
rough opening

4 1/2" wide x 6'

4 1/4 x 5:

Step #14
Once the Bookcase box is mounted and swings freely its time to mount molding to wall. This molding will hide shims and extra space required to allow box to hinge. We used bottom molding squares then fluted molding up each side as shown. The top was capped with a piece of 1" pine and than crown molding added as a finishing touch.

*** 1 1/4" Space ***   3/4" Frame   sheetrock

7 3/4"

2x4   2x8

3/4" overhang

Molding is mounted to frame and overhangs bookcase by 3/4"

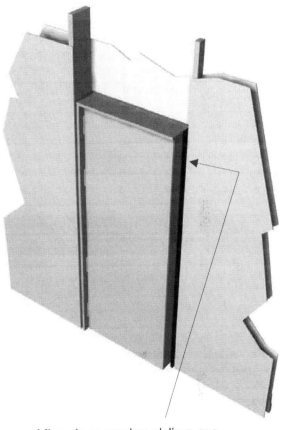

Image above shows Bookcase door with molding in place.

Left images shows front view. Right images shows back view.

After door and molding are installed you can add a block of wood to act as a stop. With door closed place block in position and mark placement. Secure with wood screws. This will prevent the door from contacting molding each time it is closed. You can also attach a magnetic latch to this same block.

The Complete Guide with detailed plans for building your own Secret Bookcase Door.

Secret Bookcase Door

www.homesafetytoday.net

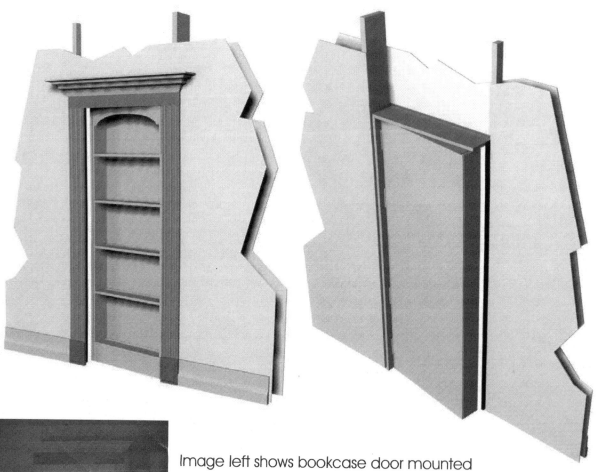

Image left shows bookcase door mounted with molding in place. Unit still needs a coat of paint, but is otherwise finished.

Image Right shows how bookcase door is overlapped by molding. Molding is attached to frame.

The Complete Guide with detailed plans for building your own Secret Bookcase Door.

Secret Bookcase Door

Picture frame hidden door built using same construction techniques. This door is actually the entrance into an attic storage space.

The Complete Guide with detailed plans for building your own Secret Bookcase Door.

Secret Bookcase Door
www.homesafetytoday.net

Finished Product.
Standard hidden bookcase door entrance.
Photos by Dan Berg

The Complete Guide with detailed plans for building your own Secret Bookcase Door.

Secret Bookcase Door
www.homesafetytoday.net

Finished Product.
Small hidden bookcase window frame attic
entrance. Photos by Dan Berg

The Complete Guide with detailed plans for building your own Secret Bookcase Door.

Other books by Daniel Berg

Ultimate Guide to Home Security

The Ultimate Guide to Home Security, by Dan Berg, Your complete guide to locks, alarms, cameras and security systems designed to protect homeowners and their valuables. This book is available as an inexpensive instant-download that you can print today and read again and again
Downloadable PDF e-book
http://www.homesafetytoday.net/

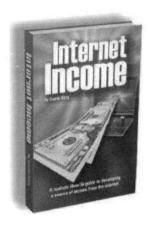

Internet Income

A realistic how to guide to developing a source of income from the internet. By Daniel Berg
This 6x9 80 page text is packed with information and loaded with illustrations. The author shows you step by step how to set up your own profit producing website. He invites you to check out working examples of each technique. The author did not develop his system for creating internet income overnight. Over the past ten years he has constantly expanded and refined a variety of internet profit centers. Mr. Berg has now complied all of his tricks of the trade into this realistic how to guide. Unlike other web profit programs Mr. Berg makes no grandiose claims. He shows readers how he has and continues to create internet income and how you can do the same.
http://www.webmoneyexpo.com/

The Complete Guide with detailed plans for building your own Secret Bookcase Door.

Secret Bookcase Door

www.homesafetytoday.net

Notes:

Secret Bookcase Door

Notes: